I dedicate this book to all those who understands the importance of daily devotion and quiet times of meditation. Your destiny is walked out through being consistent with managing a healthy life style and part of that is being fit mentally and emotionally.

This journal is designed with friendly reminders for you to take time to meditate, journal and reflect on your life's experiences ... here goes to an awesome journey!!!

Empower Me Enterprise LLC

Jacksonville, NC 28540

Published Edition October 2023

ISBN: 979-8-9893180-3-2

Cover Photo Credits: Mr. Okasha

Editor: Tracey Miller

Copyright (c) 2023 Tracey Miller

All Rights Reserved

31 Day Prayer Journal

By: Tracey Miller

Remember to learn a new skill.

Week 1

Romans 12:2

Do not be conformed to this world, but be transformed by the renewal of your mind, that by testing you may discern what is the will of God, what is good and acceptable and perfect.

MONDAY

Today is a good day to declutter all of the thoughts and cares of this world and not allow things to overwhelm you. Find your favorite quiet place and make sure you frequent it at least two or three times a week.

It helps to have this prayer journal along with the dialogue pad in order to take notes to insure you record what comes to mind.

This is the time and space where witty ideas and inventions comes to mind.

_____

_____

_____

_____

_____

_____

_____

_____

_____

_____

_____

_____

_____

TUESDAY

James 2:14-18

What good is it, my brothers, if someone says he has faith but does not have works? Can that faith save him? If a brother or sister is poorly clothed and lacking in daily food, and one of you says to them, "Go in peace, be warmed and filled," without giving them the things needed for the body, what good is that? So also, faith by itself, if it does not have works, is dead. But someone will say, "You have faith and I have works." Show me your faith apart from your works, and I will show you my faith by my works.

WEDNESDAY

Think and act on what you can do to help someone else in the time of need since the poor we will have with us always. With that being said there will always be an opportunity to give, help and support.

Get involved with the local church or organization that are providing services to help change and impact lives for the better.

What are the things that you have and are not using that can be a solution to someone else's problem?

You will discover that you have more than enough to help someone else.

_____

_____

_____

_____

_____

_____

_____

_____

_____

_____

_____

_____

THURSDAY

Matthew 6:22-23

The eye is the lamp of the body. So, if your eye is healthy, your whole body will be full of light, but if your eye is bad, your whole body will be full of darkness. If then the light in you is darkness, how great is the darkness!

FRIDAY

The eyes tell the story. Be mindful of what you focus on and give attention too. Remember, its really how you handle what you see that matters the most. At times we will see things that are disturbing or discouraging and other times we will see things that are good and enlightening. So what are you focusing on.

Looking someone strait in the eye may state in some cultures that you are paying attention and don't have anything to hide or that you are an honest person while in other cultures it is looked on as a disrespect. Whatever your culture lets share and enlighten yourself and others with joy and good experiences as well as memories.

_____

_____

_____

_____

_____

_____

_____

_____

_____

_____

_____

_____

SATURDAY

1 John 2:10

The one who loves his brother abides in the Light and there is no cause for stumbling in him.

SUNDAY

Enhance your critical thinking.

Week 2

We must remember to love ourselves in order to love one another and when we are operating in the true love there will be no room for competition or jealously. A heart full of love and compassion will have a desire to love, help and support others.

No man is an island. It takes a team of people to get things done. We may not be on the same team at all times or the same time. It is important to be respectful and supportive as much as possible

The individual that tries to stop a plan or work have not come into or walking towards their purpose stay focused and don't get distracted. Keep working and moving forward to accomplish your goals.

_____

_____

_____

_____

_____

_____

_____

_____

_____

_____

_____

MONDAY

Genesis 1:27

So God created man in his own image, in the image of God created he him; male and female created he them.

TUESDAY

Jeremiah 29:11

For I know the thoughts that I think toward you, saith the LORD, thoughts of peace, and not of evil, to give you an expected end.

You are not an accident, your life has purpose, everything that we go through will be used the good, bad and the ugly nothing will be wasted. At times you may not understand the process. Let me encourage you to keep living and persevere any hardships or curve balls life throws your way

WEDNESDAY

Psalms 91:1-2

He who dwells in the shelter of the Most High will abide in the shadow of the Almighty. I will say to the Lord, He is my refuge and my fortress, my God, in whom I trust.

THURSDAY

We will be kept and provided for at all times in spite the times when we have to deal with situations that seem too impossible to bear. Reflecting back over past experiences at the time is seemed like the worst and that it would never end and then you look up and you are out of it and there has been a way made.

It is in those times that we are really growing and learning. We learn to be more strategic and for some people even the creativity kicks in. I like to call this the worst of times that helps create the best of times. Remember there is no victory without a challenge.

_____

_____

_____

_____

_____

_____

_____

_____

_____

_____

_____

_____

FRIDAY

John 15:4

Abide in Me, and I in you. As the branch cannot bear fruit of itself unless it abides in the vine, so neither can you unless you abide in Me

SATURDAY

*There is no greater intimacy than with God.
The best time is to spend time with the one who created you.
He knows everything about you and will never change his mind or love for you.*

*He is the one that can heal you every where.
You don't have to be afraid to receive his love, guidance or direction.
He knows what's best. So today is a good day to spend quiet time with him.*

_____
_____
_____
_____
_____
_____
_____
_____
_____
_____
_____
_____
_____
_____

SUNDAY

Eating is essential to good health.

Week 3

Romans 15:13

Now the God of hope fill you with all joy and peace in believing that ye may abound in hope, through the power of the Holy Ghost.

MONDAY

*Never loose your hope and you will keep your joy.
Laughter strengthens you and music sets that atmosphere for joy.*

It wont erase the things that you are faced with, however, it will help change your mind in how you see things.

So, remember to laugh a little it will carry you a long way.

TUESDAY

Psalms 103:10-12

He has not dealt with us according to our sins, nor punished us according to our iniquities. For as the heavens are high above the earth, so great is His mercy toward those who fear Him; as far as the east is from the west, so far has He removed our transgressions from us.

WEDNESDAY

You have heard it said that when you hold on to hurt and unforgiveness it's like you drinking the poison and expecting the person that offended you to be hurt by it.

Never let the actions or opinions of others control your life.

Have a forgiving heart. It will certainly set you apart and you will lead the way to the most precious gift which is Love.

Remember, we are creatures of habit and at times the person might not even be aware of the behavior.

In order to move forward you must let go of what is behind you.

THURSDAY

1 Corinthians 13:4-5

Love is patient, love is kind. It does not envy, it does not boast, it is not proud. It does not dishonor others, it is not self-seeking, it is not easily angered, it keeps no record of wrongs

FRIDAY

If you ever want to know if you are operating in Love this scripture is what I'd like to say a check list ask yourself these questions

Have I been patient today?

Have I shown kindness to others?

Am I comparing Myself to others?

Did I operate in a spirit of pride?

Have I dishonored others?

Did I make today all about me?

Have I allowed myself to be easily angered?

Am I keeping a record of others wrong doings?

If so take the time to work on a better you to help shape a greater tomorrow.

SATURDAY

John 15:16

You did not choose Me but I chose you, and appointed you that you would go and bear fruit, and that your fruit would remain, so that whatever you ask of the Father in My name He may give to you.

SUNDAY

Physical activity can support longevity.

Week 4

Although things happen that are not planned or expected that does not take away your purpose in life the path that we take and the hurdles that we have to jump over are just that.

Destiny is calling while life is shaping you. Just remember, don't turn into sour grapes in the process. Learn to apply the sugar to the areas in life when needed so that your fruit in life is sweet and pleasant.

_____

_____

_____

_____

_____

_____

_____

_____

_____

_____

_____

_____

_____

MONDAY

Philippians 1:6

And I am sure of this, that he who began a good work in you will bring it to completion at the day of Jesus Christ

TUESDAY

Does not mean that you ignore that you had a past it simply means not to dwell on it to the point that you become paralyzed and unable to move forward.

Our past announces that we have grown or that we need to grow, change and mature.

The lessons and experiences of our past is the foundation of our future, in fact the past prepares us for what is ahead. The things that are current in our life at this very moment is also preparing us for our tomorrow every step, time and season in our life just never get stuck in one season because they all have meaning.

_____
_____
_____
_____
_____
_____
_____
_____
_____
_____
_____
_____
_____

WEDNESDAY

Exodus 33:14

My presence shall go with you and I will give you rest.

THURSDAY

There is nothing like the presence of God, you will experience peace on another level.

You smile just because and in spite of it all.

Things become clearer to you.

When you are one with the creator you are complete.

You become emotionally healthier.

Remember your peace is priceless and anything that would interrupt your peace must be removed because having no peace is detrimental to you.

Love you because you matter.

FRIDAY

I Peter 2:9

But you are a chosen people, a royal priesthood, a holy nation, God's special possession, that you may declare the praises of him who called you out of darkness into his wonderful light.

SATURDAY

There are times that you have to excuse yourself from anything and anybody that try to minimize who you are as an individual.

At times we can get caught up in helping others that we forget that we have to nurture and take care of ourselves.

Never settle for anything less that the best and you can have it especially because you give your best.

_____

_____

_____

_____

_____

_____

_____

_____

_____

_____

_____

_____

_____

_____

SUNDAY

Prayer and meditation promotes peace.

Week 5

Deuteronomy 31:6

*Be strong and courageous. Do not be afraid or terrified because of them, for the L*ord *your God goes with you; he will never leave you nor forsake you.*

MONDAY

Matthew 28:20

Teaching them to observe all things whatsoever I have commanded you: and, lo, I am with you always, even unto the end of the world. Amen.

TUESDAY

In those times or days when you feel all alone and the house might be crowded but you feel all alone.

Remember God is there when it seems that no one else cares.

He not only hears your cries but he knows exactly what's on your mind.

Focus on the positives and reflect on the good times.

It will help to clear your mind.

_____

_____

_____

_____

_____

_____

_____

_____

_____

_____

_____

_____

_____

WEDNESDAY

Made in the USA
Columbia, SC
27 July 2025